Goodnight
from Heaven

— all about you —

colleen bishop

Goodnight from Heaven
Copyright © 2021 by Colleen Bishop

Tellwell Talent
www.tellwell.ca

ISBN
978-0-2288-4314-6 (Hardcover)
978-0-2288-4315-3 (Paperback)

All About You

Here we are, all ready for bed.

You're all tucked in, just rest your head.

And while you lay there, all cozy and warm,

I want to tell you about who you are.

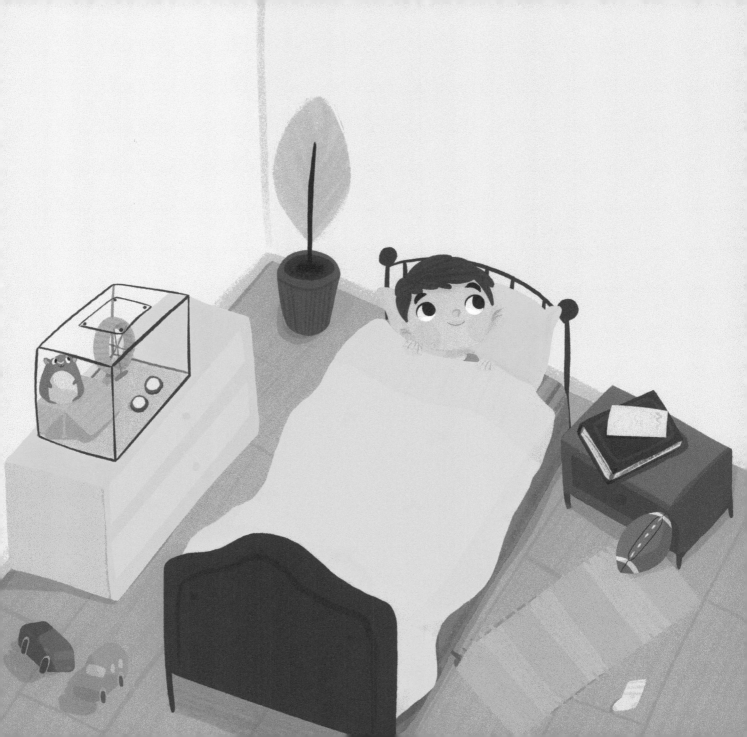

So, my sweet one...

Make sure that you listen and make sure that you hear.

Take these words in and hold each one near.

You're someone important!

You're someone who's loved!

You're someone who deserves a million 99 hugs!

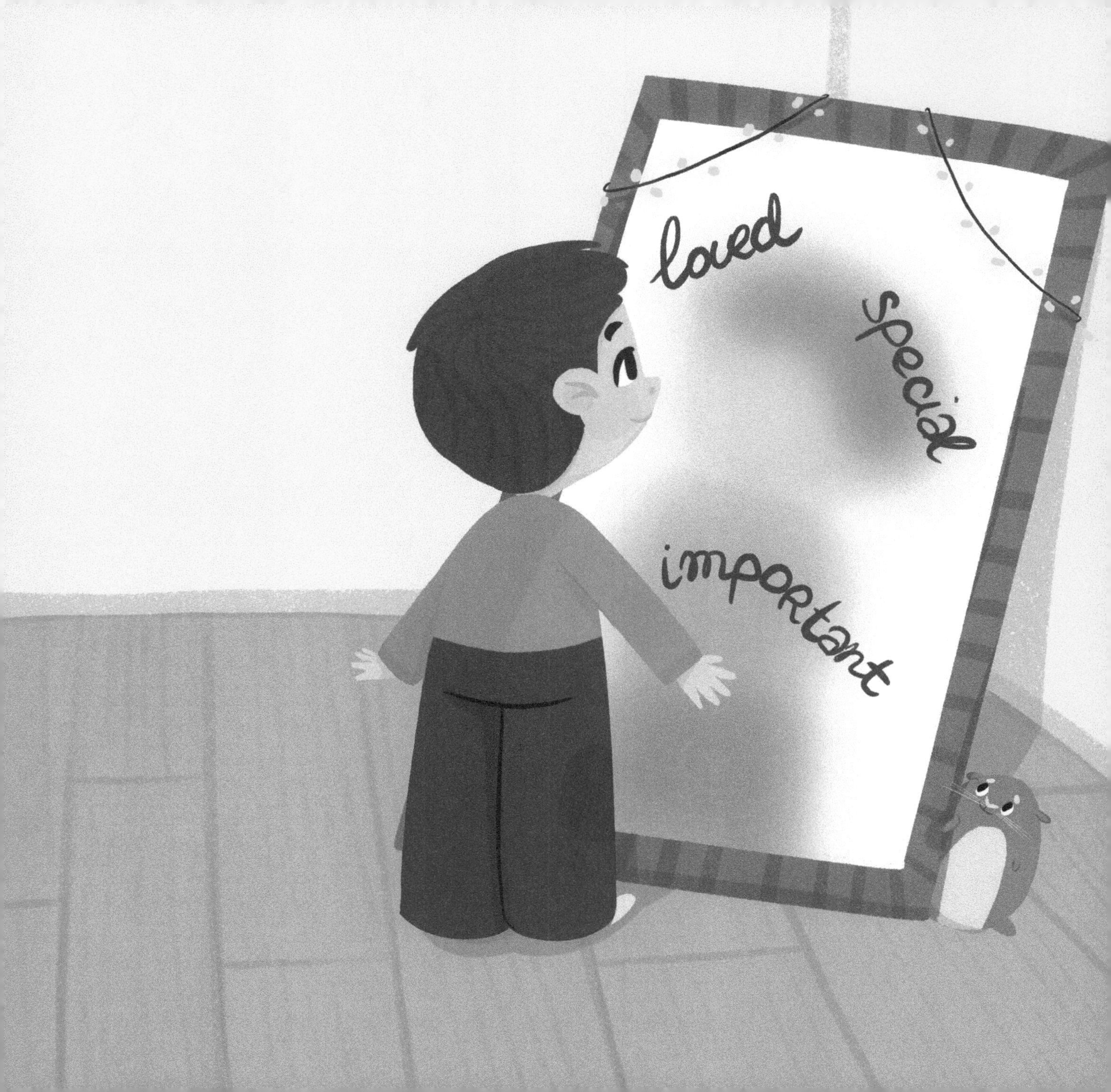
loved
special
important

You were made SPECIAL, as anyone can see.

And you are a SPECIAL part of your family.

There are SO many people who care about you!

And, guess what?

You also have a Father up in Heaven. . . it's true!!

He is a great King and He sits on a Throne.

A sparkly and comfy, big place of His own.

This King that I speak of, He's Mighty and True.

And He would do anything... anything for you!

He's FILLED with love.

And He's FILLED with smiles.

And He wants you to know...

His Big Love for you will never get tired.

Mighty God

Wonderful   Everlasting

Counselor   Father

Prince of Peace

He's placed in your heart, all that you need

To grow, to be strong, and to live happily.

And as a surprise, for you to see

He's created other things to help you believe.

is this good ? ? ?

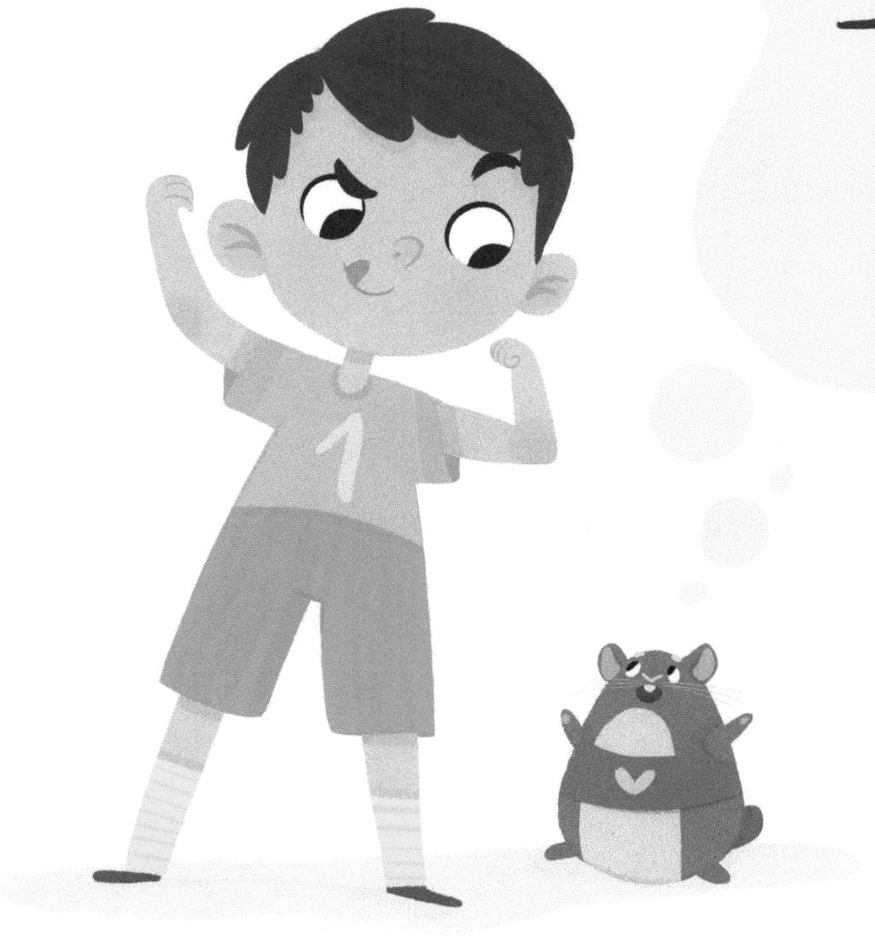

He says...

"Do you see all those stars, the ones way up high?

I made every one, and they twinkle like My Eyes.

I made the moon and I made the sun.

I made trees and butterflies and elephants that weigh 3 tons!"

"Yes, it's true, I have made many things.

But there's only one thing that really makes My Heart sing.

It's YOU! You're My favorite! My Heart's greatest delight!

You're My child, and I love you with all of My Might."

"So, My sweet one...

I want you to know, I want you to see

How SPECIAL you are to your family and Me.

You're someone important!

You're someone who's loved!

You're someone who deserves a million 99 hugs!"

"So, whenever you wonder about who you are,

Just look at the sky and up to the stars.

Watch for a twinkle and then know that it's Me,

Saying, 'I see you, my child, you're part of My big family!'"

"Now close your eyes and drift off to sleep.

I'm on My Throne taking care of everything.

Goodnight from Heaven...

Goodnight, my sweet."

CPSIA information can be obtained
at www.ICGtesting.com
Printed in the USA
BVHW062132220821
614828BV00003B/42

9 780228 843145

Winston
Takes a Me Day
by
Sarah Roach

Published by eBookIt.com
http://www.eBookIt.com

ISBN-13: 978-1-4566-3872-6

For Wallie
in memory
of Tedd

Winston woke up at 6:00 am on Monday morning and instantly knew something was not right. His brain felt foggy, his body felt groggy, and he was sad.

"Mama?" he said as he slowly walked into his parent's bedroom. "I think I might need to take a 'me day'. I'm not feeling so rad".

"That's alright Winston" his mama said slowly. "It's okay to not be okay. Let's do some self care and take a me day."

Mama put on her sweater, gave Winston a kiss, checked the note from the therapist, and turned on the calming music playlist.

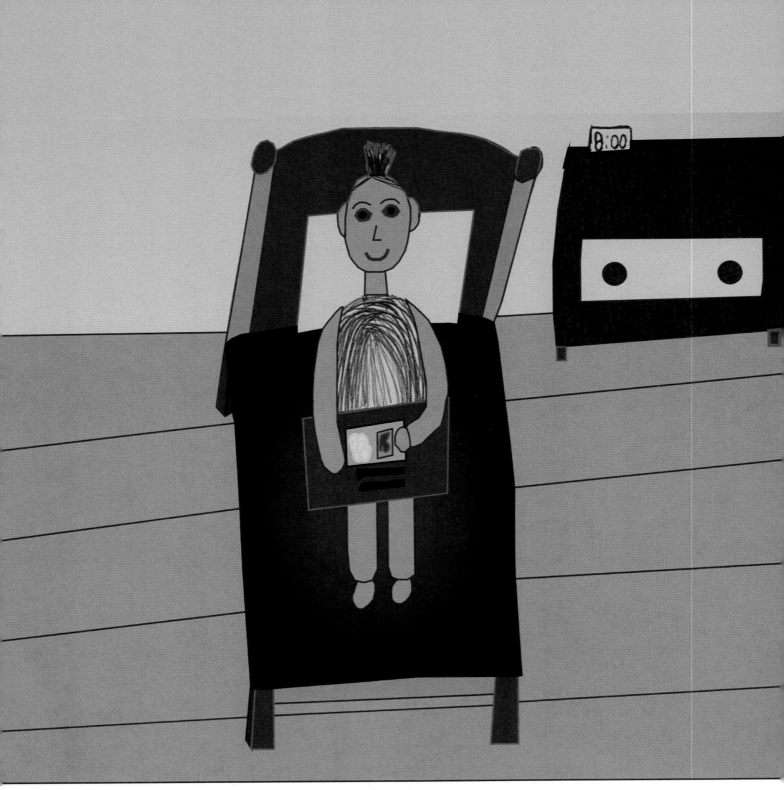

First on the agenda was breakfast in bed. Mental health can be hard, but it helps to be fed.

Next up Winston talked to his
therapist on Zoom. Dr. Liz is so good,
it felt like she was in the room.

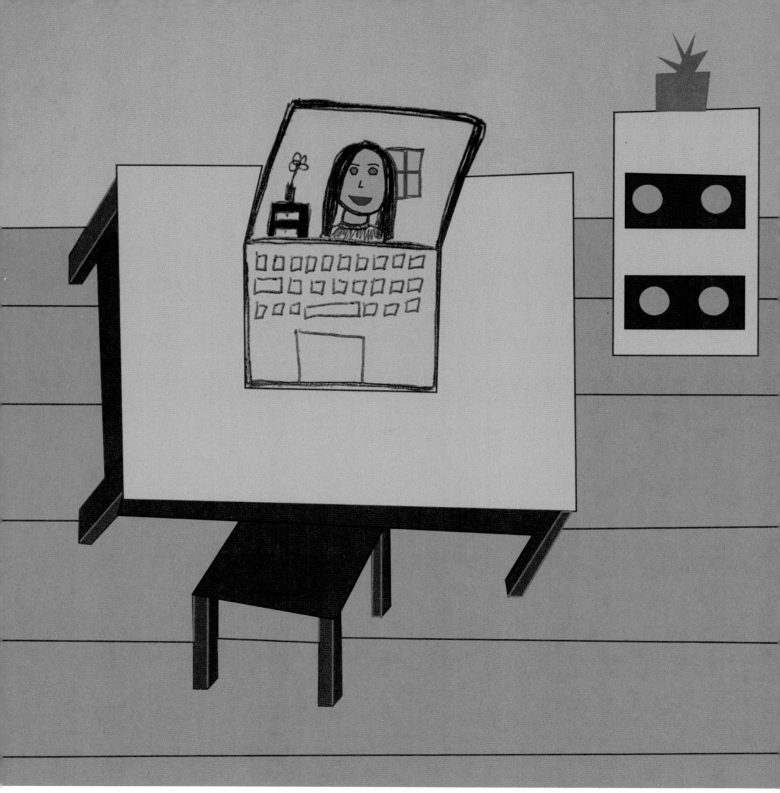

After some exercises and a fun game about feelings, Winston was ready for some outdoor healing.

I'm starting to feel better" Winston said after a walk. "My brain is less foggy, and it felt good to talk!"

"That's great!" said Mama. "I'm happy you're well! But if you feel down again, do you know who to tell?"

"You!" exclaimed Winston "or Dr. Liz, or my teacher, because it's okay to not be okay, and that doesn't make me any weaker!"

Made in the USA
Coppell, TX
19 February 2022

73802227R00017